Drive

Drive

Elaine Sexton

Grid Books BOSTON

GRID BOOKS
Boston, Massachusetts
grid-books.org

COVER:
Early Morning Swim, 2020
Katherine Bradford
Gouache on paper
14 × 11 inches

AUTHOR PHOTO:
Courtesy of Marina Kiriakou

Printed by Cushing Malloy
Ann Arbor, Michigan

ISBN: 978-1-946830-14-2

for Nora

CONTENTS

Drive

The most beautiful thing about my car is the beach, and the most beautiful thing about the beach is watercolor, and the most beautiful thing about water is the word, and the most beautiful thing about the word is pigment, and the most beautiful thing about pigment is the soil, and the most beautiful thing about soil is the earth, and the most beautiful thing about the earth is the sea, and the most beautiful thing about the sea is the drive.

I.

This

for H.S.

In the way your poem
with a lake in it
is not about the lake, mine
with a dog and the broken
heart is not about a dog
or saving face. Your ibis as pearls
in their nests is no more
about the sway of banyan trees
than it is about lovers and brothers
or fathers living among
the cedars
and scat in my poems, nor
those pyres by the tracks
waiting for a match, all
queerly remembered, queer
as teaching ourselves
not to drown, or of clouds
that don't move, what a sea hawk
carries in her talons,
and the long dirt road,
and the navel of the moon?
All poems about storms at sea,
combined, are not about
the earth's proclivities, but
deciding what spins.
Everything is about
gravity, the grave
pulling
for us. Each day
it starts with a bark
calling our name.

Caper

When I am an eraser I can do
  anything. Mistakes may be made
with impunity. I write
  as though paper will never be
priceless, it crumples
  and springs back. The invention
of the pencil protects me
  from permanency and
practicality. Ideas are not
  commitments. This jaw line
may be drawn smooth, not
  cracked, to receive a caress.
I draw shade and under it
  a neck, shoulders. I dream
this to be me, that dreams
  matter. If I can be my dream,
and live it too, so can you.

The Motorist

"Life is a movie. Death is a photograph."
Susan Sontag

A picture of a car and its driver
competes poorly
with the road, the cliff, the sea

moving,
in real time. Between the driver
and her heap,

her free arm open,
her hand is catching and letting go
atoms and atoms of that

which shall remain
nameless
so long as she knows

she is free not to be
where she's expected to go.

Drive

My tiny car's tiny engine
groans and hums
the way my mother hummed

a little ditty when
nervous,
the way I do

mulling over something hard
letting my chest
send a message

to my mouth, my mouth
forming a kind of growl
while all along

staying shut. I enter
the on-ramp to the freeway
heading home

from a family visit,
the pedal to the floor,
I pump my chin

toward the dashboard
thinking I'm helping.
I think I hear

my brother's taunt:
What is it
with women

and cars? We are old,
old enough,
to equate mobility

with independence.
Real wheels
take me out of state,

escaping the trap
I thought was
the small town. For this

I left the ocean
I left the trees
I left Eel Pond with seabirds

standing on spring ice,
summer surfboards lined up
on the berm

between the sea grass
and the sea.
I left my family of origin,

my Lucky buried in the back-
yard, dog heaven,
now home to a chalet

built by strangers,
the chicken coop,
the barn, gone. When

driving I think of love
as a road trip, the soaring,
the breakdown, jump-

starts, the brand new,
and old reliable.
I'm no mechanic

though I once knew
how to change a fan belt
sheared to a thread.

Here the air is fresh.
The new mutt
who travels with me

leaves her nose prints
on the passenger windows
the way my old dog did,

leaving a spot
just clear enough
to drive through.

Run

I am walking &
talking at first
then humming
picking up the pace

my stride following
the singing which
begins as a
strum

until a clicking
reminds me that fuel
which is matter
which is mind

which is idea
is not endless
and only as fertile
as the working

brain
allows—
the brain we take
for granted

which could fail
at any time.
And that
clicking?

I begin
to walk faster
unused to
the acceleration

of unknowing
how to keep up
with losing
a fading of something

that is not firm
graspable
watching it go
a voice which is

now
singing
as if voice were light
and the sun is

that shot
in the dark
that cries
run.

Self-Portrait: Between the Car and the Sea

I think I'll stay blonde
a while longer. Downshifting
for the view, today,

the engine strains
in first gear the way
on foot my body

climbing the last few steps
does. You'd hear it, too,
if the heart

had a literal voice. Silently
pulling for itself,
the will wants the body to

give it what it wants.
How long will these parts last?
I put off minding the flags

lifting their faces. I watch sea lice flit
from shell to sand to beach
eased by transition lenses.

Inventory

This is the blade that wipes
the glass that clears the rain/
snow/leaves that

cuts the chemical
mix that cuts the salt
mud from the road that clouds

the curved surface
conceived to bend.
And stays that way

to let the wind
glide over it.
All of this and none of this

is metaphor for what
is seen through,
the direct

experience of which
is delayed just enough
to allow

eyed, eared,
nosed, lipped—
expression,

something
the body shows
but not as clear

as the head.

Fuel

My stealth self
wants to know
what I am driving at

when I say *drive.* I idle,
touching the ignition
now that a car

needs no key,
no handler,
not even

me. I reach for the stick
shift, the hand-
break, the choke,

retrieve an imaginary
clutch. No passenger
knows

what a driver knows,
her grip
on the wheel, foot

on the pedal,
flat
to the floor. My hand

to eye equals
foot to gut
coordination. Speed

equals oxygen
to the brain. The dead
ends of my hair

dragged through the air,
pull their roots
alive. Did she say

or did I say
drive?

Ignition

I remember my hand
on the car's smooth blue

lining, the Rambler's
door as it opened

to the damp grass
of the lawn

to the new house.
I was three

close to four
years old, my father,

newly dead
and my mother

just learning
to drive.

How to Draw a Heart

The arteries of the turbine as seen from the
train are actively compressing *god knows what*
as we shuttle past Deer Park Station. I think
I read it was jet fuel to fuel engines, and jet
engine components produced here, parts as
small as the smallest rotors for dental drills
to full-scale motor armatures like those of the
heart, which is as close to a turbine as any-
thing else in the body. I guess the stomach,
too, is a turbine but I don't see the stomach
illustrated on any Hallmark cards, no doily-
accompanied tubes to say *I love you* though
the stomach is really the first to know if
something's up before the heart kicks in, the
engines to the intimate holding infinitely
complex hinges that swing with desire. We
keep trying to illustrate desire as if desire were
something one could draw as an expression of
love, something possible to construct.

Nonplace

That spring before I met you
I found myself
in a tiny white rental car
with a moon-roof
and stick shift
in a country where
I didn't speak
the language
on a roadway
whose names and numbers
didn't match
my Baedeker
nor the *quaint* idea
to bring a map
that belonged to my father
who died
young.

And I could swear
he joined me
skirting foothills
we explored
decades earlier
on a family trip
in an American Oldsmobile
abroad
though I have no way
to prove we drove
this same route.

Maybe the past is not
the way to navigate. So strong
the impulse
to make place
personal. But this was it
my non-
place
the off hours
days alone

my body blessed
with little significance
without lover without friends
no family
nor possibility
of conversation
so little familiar

even the gas pump presented
a craving for intelligence
a marker
coming and going
craving and
caving
heaven on earth
coming
and for god's sake
going.

Copper Beech

Because it had been, quite literally,
four decades since I last climbed a tree
I stood a long while watching you
overhead. Your elbows disappeared
in the sheets of plum-dark leaves,
so cool in the heat. I pressed
my face against the bark, I patted
your dog's snout—lost—my body touching
the idea of leaving earth. I wrapped
my arms around a trunk wider than
my own, growth and decay in my mouth.
I kissed the twins, fear and ecstasy,
my feet where my shoulders
once were. My fingers reached
for the sole of your shoe. A blanket of green
held me in its arms, the backsides
of leaves last seen from the ground.

sin·gle·ton

My friend says he's sure he'll run across one
walking his dog in the cool green Fells across the road.

They climb to their lookout, each day, different,
the same. Homer will dive into Boston's drinking water

reservoir to fetch a stick, one of a kind, one of many dogs
fetching sticks in the cold deep, held by granite and gravel,

close to the single longest day of the year. I climb out
of one of my selves, looking for another way

to go at the day. Solo. We are born this way.
How keen it must be to be twinned from the start,

always in tandem with another flesh-and-blood other,
unlike the rest of us watching the wrist of our thinking

fling dreams over a pool without a tide.

Predator / Bait

The whole thing, over
in a flash. One splash

follows another.
She is pulling up

the anchor and I am gathering
the lines, fishing

then swimming. Sorry
for the fish and glad

to be alive. I say this—*glad
to be alive*—at least

once a day,
when it doesn't rain,

when the Tiffany-blue
egg isn't snatched

from the nest
constructed too close

to the ground. Each day,
one chick less. This week

a tiny yellow beak
opened so wide *hope*

is a fly. As today
in the bay, for the fish

that gets away, a splash
is just a splash.

Mussels

We steam them open,
like injured fans,
their fleshy throats
exposed. We would
find it hard to eat anything if we let

all that ever lived
remain
untouched—
the flat-faced flounder,
dug from the sea,

the eggplant,
clipped from the vine,
the perfect egg, worried
from the womb
of the hen, and the hen herself.

I slice a star fruit open
and the gel, sweet and good,
glistens, giving shape
to appetite.
Shall we fast? Ignore

the trot of the rabbit,
the plain-faced
pomme frites, rose-colored radishes
their feathered tops,
creme fraiche,

the origin of butter, the origin
of bread for the elegant meal?
What of the grapes,
ripening, then picked?
What of that?

[ride]

The most beautiful thing about a convertible is hair, and the most beautiful thing about hair is its disposition, dead, but alive in the skin in the air, the skin holding on to each strand for dear life, alive in the wind. The most beautiful thing about the wind passing over the skin is sensation, cellular, invisible, metabolic. What is metabolic is life-sustaining, and the most life-sustaining thing I can think of today is decency. And decency is blind, unseen, until it isn't.

Oh!

You again, I think,
framing my thoughts
to align with where

my body has brought me
today, in the flick
of a peacock's neck, one of a pair

pecking the lawn
yards away
from where I sit

with a new love and old
friends. Back
in the conversation

I am having with myself,
so strange
the way two tall birds

now lying prone
on their chests
as though swimming

in the grass, their stick legs
pinned back,
are calling you. Odd enough

to be in their company
as well as that of a pink
flamingo keeping time

with the mariachi band,
her head knocking
back and forth

in time with three guitarists.
But it is you, here, now,
a little less

menacing,
supplicant,
human scale,

as vivid a blue
as will ever be found
in nature.

A Thing or Two

The leaf falls on the page,
red after being green

her whole life. The mail carrier
and his broken marriage

at the door deliver grief
and the *Paris Review,*

the icemaker knocking out
ice. Outside the trees laugh

the tops of their heads off.
This blow, a breeze, gusts

wildly denuding
deciduous trees, determined

to leave nothing weak behind.
Oblivious, the pines

have grown too close
to the shingled house.

They brush the slats.
Both are cedar and flirt

with reunification. We live
by the sea and clear-cut trees

harvested for building
and burning. Some die

for others, and by some
I mean those who don't breathe

the way we do, but are no less
alive: beach grass, trees, the breeze.

Dear trees—the earth still spins
for the love of you. I lean my skin

against your skin. My dog
in all innocence pees

at your feet. I let him.
Your mourning arouses—x—

in the air, what I breathe
and can't breathe,

what I see and don't—but want to.

Latin for Nothing

We adjust our eyes to the dim
horizon, to the lights
on the causeways

across the Sound. All week
I work on nothing. Nothing
is the new subject, the new
economy. Now, with time

to consider it, time herself
dwindles, retreats,
resilio, Latin for dwindle,
shrinks, and springs back. Time

resilient, always there
but often diminished, always
dwindling, except
in the abstract.

II.

Transport

I don't expect the end
to be like the din of a river,
a sound
with no beginning.

I'm certain the end is the sea.
Not the sound of the sea,
but the sea itself,
the part that expires

after it heaves. You
may think the sea draws a breath
and comes back, but
the *what* of it ends

in a wave. There is an end
to a wave. That's my view,
my range, those are my thoughts
as they downshift from sky

to road to sea in a Fiat
which struggles to power
its way into Spain
over the steep pitch

of the coast road, the nervous
gear-shift clicking in such a way
I begin to wonder
where I left my Last Will

& Testament. Cresting each peak,
I conjure the names
of my family of friends on signage
before the road drops

into the perfect dark O
blasted into a neck
of a cliff, reeling
from black out back into the light,

into the vineyards, perpendicular
to the one-lane highway,
the grape leaves so close
they graze the car's door

skirting sharp curves,
as I become the sea
become the horizon.
Driving alone

voices in my head
wait to be heard,
those dying to speak,
enter the car

the windows wide open:
I can't believe
you chose this road
one says. Another's

matches the twiggy vines
knotted
in the dry brown earth
like ties to a quilt. One

counts syllables,
sensory signals on signposts
in three languages
whizzing by. Another

searches the rear-view
mirror, thinking out loud:
watch that biker
cycling too close to the car.

When the GPS enters
the conversation,
my voices
jam behind a jack-knifed truck—

KAFKA TRANSPORT S.A.—
in block letters on its cab—
a voice suggests we turn back
five kilometers.

I see what the GPS
cannot. She,
with the British accent
and satellite vectors:

this detour is really a path.
Can I still fix a flat? I ask
the empty car
trying to remember

the last vehicle…the last person
passed after leaving
the paved roads. Alone (together)
we climb a ridge

that had been blocking the view
all along, behind which
are white-capped hilltops
a vast valley, unpassable

below. The window open,
I feel for the air, sweet and slow.
Daylight pours over my face,
my lap. I thank then curse

no one, backing up
a few thousand yards,
skidding and dipping
spilling the useless

map, notes, water
from a cup. I imagine
my hair at a slant, cartoon-
style, watching my wallet

slide out of sight. *Alone*
and in a circumstance
without losing my way
my shirt might

still be dry, but I might never
have considered a soft
fall from a cliff,
among poppies

so red they recompose red
in vines so faint they are
practically white,
so tangled they conjugate

the verb *to tangle*
a new way, the way
green tangles into
the crease of the rocks,

the way the Mediterranean
tangles into cloud cover
turning a shade
that could never be made

by hand. I see
how the road ruts now,
the way it twists
as I backed

all the way down
to a seedy town, taking
time, something I can
handle and untangle, here,

now, without a watch.

Next

after Ray Johnson

When a word looks like
it wants to eat the one
that comes after it

what comes next
inevitably
pushes it along.

The window
pushed opened
let the trapped bee

walk out. And a house fly
with, possibly,
an hour left to live,

followed it
as the light faltered
and moisture

gathered in the trees.

Now

The sun is driving my car
whose top

is peeled halfway back,
so my dog's nose

is pitched straight up. And
though I am recovering

from a cold, the heat
and the motionless sky

have convinced me
I need fresh air

in my lungs. My lungs
remain mute, but not so

the crows in the reeds
who tower over the two of us

(me, the dog) in the low-slung car
stopped on Narrow River Road,

what's not really a river
but a slender estuary

leading to the bay, where
great swathes of Canada Geese

paddled to see us
in a V shape

the way they fly. Tame?
I would say: *curious*.

I was a little nervous,
my young pup so small

he looked like bait. Soon,
in pods of five or six

or eight, then a dozen cut out
over the fields over our heads,

and disappeared
to join the crows gathered

here. When we stop, our windows
come down to listen to

the geese and crows arguing,
agreeing, complaining,

almost human their confusion
over what to do now.

Landscape with Power Lines

The twisting chords, no longer
bother me. As I see it,
they heighten the light, halved

and halved again, leaves and clouds, snow
and storm. The breeze moves an olive branch
over one line, then another below. Each branch

acts as if her leaves aren't about to be swayed
to stay on one side for good. They remain
undecided. Today they are subject to a dust

kicked up as a truck hauling crops powers past.
Birds make their wild plans to nest
one last time. They weave their sticks

and tissue their housing
including these lines.
We are bound to live together.

Still Life Inside Last Year's Chinese Lanterns

If pigment works the way memory does
the flowers from the vine
break their old frames open
each October knowing
next year more blossoms
will come. More balloon than flower,
each weighs next to nothing, they fit,
left to right, in the small of my palms.

Picked, they pay a price for their beauty
with what's left of their life.

Let me add to this picture: broken open
tiny red nubs, blood red seeds
stand on stems, dead center.
In good soil they might
anchor to earth. The light will intensify
their come-back colors: pumpkin and plum,
colors you can almost see
from this description.

Artificial Intelligence

Forget about cyborgs
the chopper

stalled over my building
is spasm of recall brought

to life as the shell of your
voice

leaving me   for good

& could never be
artificially reproduced

not with Stelarc's
surgically constructed

third ear, not with intra-
ocular lenses

giving a second
sight to the blinded-by-

eros among us   Face it

the moth with integrated
electronics

installed in her thorax

has no more
self determination

than a gnat   And will char
to a bulb

sooner than
I can conjure

a defibrillator to jump start
this drone aimed at

object-oriented language
minimizing loss

and the logic of capital
maximizing profit

which is the song
capitalists must sing

if they are to make
their way

with straw for thoughts
to where love lives

with a match,
without touch,

waiting to be lit.

Old. Rome.

I was walking and chipping at an idea
of two monuments to commerce,
of aging, of beauty, of the Vatican,
of Gagosian. Between one famous piazza
and my hotel, in the clean light
of a one-room shop,
an old man handled a small head
broken open on a table, both head and table
the color of dust. Plasters & figures,
clocks filled the shelves. The bust,
a larger than life-size woman
with carved hair, cossetted and colorless,
her one elbow, intact, leaned over
the artworker's head, hers
probably older than his, his
probably older than mine,
but just barely
older.

Girl with a Book

The book tells me
you can read,
the binding unembellished,
as secular as your dress,

plain, red, which suggests
this is not scripture
in your hands. The fact
of the halo in the fresco

makes you a saint. The painter
gave you almond eyes,
bare shoulders, an unfazed
gaze. The lapis blue wall

is your night, the century
in which you lived.
No sadness in your frame,
nor in your exposed ear.

Passengers, Assisi to Rome

To prove he had not stolen
the pink-faced teenage girl's iPhone,
my seatmate emptied his jacket
and backpack, all of it

on the floor in the aisle.
The smell of shoes and unwashed
clothes rose from the flecked linoleum
in the air over his sack

with the glint of Mediterranean almonds
and off-brand cigarettes. Partly
in Italian, partly in English
she charged: *I know Albanians*

to the silent Carabinieri.
The accused's sweat filled
the silver bullet of the train's car
blasting through the side of the mountain

at such a speed as to freeze
sunflowers in place
in the fields we passed, their backs
to the sun, not about to raise their heads.

On Rothko's "Dark Palette"

after Election Day, 2016

The suited gallery guards
usher us in. Like mourners
we gauge & weigh our pleasure

as the new climate we live in
grows grim. From this leather-
bound bench I follow a scratched

horizon crossing the canvas, cutting
pigment the color of pavement,
as our palette gets darker, then dim.

Sky Burial

I'm pinching a little
from the sky every day,
dawn to dusk.

Dug in the dirt,
the bulbs, weeds, stems,
stamen dust staining,

seed their cumulous way.
There is always the air.
I brush the mud

from my shirt, clip the dead
and dying dahlias. Your shirt,
your dahlias. Dead,

you keep what you wanted to
back. That
desire is everywhere.

The sky has her say
now that you're dust
now that you've come apart.

My Dead

brother returns as
the old man in the sea
surfing. The waves change,

but always change
in the same way. My brother
will always be a comma

in a sea of commas,
a pause in the loose
language of waves

seen from shore. He will always be
too far away to read, as close
as the salt on my skin

is—like his skin—that dries
and flakes.
And shadows him.

Anthem

His face, a flag, fades
and folds into
what it once was

in death, an anthem
to itself. He is wave
after wave of what

promised to be
a good ride. Always
in four-wheel drive,

he is passenger
and pilot, both.
The roll bar protects us

from breaking
our necks.
What I know

about him,
I know
without doors,

without windows,
without a roof.

Listening to Cement Dry

I'm stealing the sound
from the sand. I come up

with nothing. Nothing
is when walking

and waking
are one. Moss

on the tombstone, grass
listening

as it grows
over one paved date

waiting
for the right side

of a hyphen. Nothing
in between. Jackhammers

hammer the street. Everything
eye-level. Please

give that chisel a break.

Sew

The surgeon still binds
our wounds the way
cave dwellers

cinched woolly capes
and caps, viscous
and weave—

the original thread,
the first needle, pig's gut,
heron's beak chiseled

to the size of a wick
with an eye. I wonder
how my mother

seamed her desires—
her sewing, her rudder,
the hum and glow,

pedal below,
how she learned to drive,
a widow alone

in a small-town wilderness,
object-oriented. Her making
my own.

Driving

There are still dead zones
in America

where no one lives
and satellites turn a deaf ear.

It was only because of the light
leaving the sky, ice forming

on the glass of my stalled car
I entered the sedan

of a stranger, a man
who stopped on the interstate

in one of those red states
shaped like a box.

There are still strangers
who stop for a woman

in distress and think only
of her distress.

If anyone strikes me
on the street

I can return the Blow
the reclusive poet wrote

—alone
and in a circumstance—

what did she know?

One Sings, the Other Doesn't

A cento, movie titles beginning and ending with Agnés Varda

One sings stormy weather, gone
with the wind, clueless.
Miss Congeniality,
the help, the First Wives Club,
in a league of their own, wild.
She's beautiful when she's angry,
death proof. All about my mother
set it off, a girl walks home alone,
a question of silence, an unmarried woman.
Diamonds are a girl's best friend—
but are they? The women: the hours,
itty bitty titty committee, bad girl,
women without men, sweetie,
the Stepford wives, even cowgirls
get the blues. I am somebody,
if these walls could talk. Lipstick
under my burka, the little
girl who lives down the lane,
legally blonde, goddess remembered,
the love witch, born in flames, vagabond.

Lines Written While Pumping Gas

One day my assistant in sales
came to work with
a locked case,

carrying a gun for fun,
this young Republican,
blue suit, blue eyes,

clean cut. I let him
lead me to his private
club, a basement den,

and fold my fingers
around his
solid cold pistol. A real one.

Registered, I aimed
and shot a silhouette
of a man's head,

a bull's-eye. Men
and their games.
He soon left publishing

to become a broker
just before the last
crash. For weeks after

I watched the steel door
on lower Fifth,
looking for pistol

practitioners. Today,
someone who looks like him
offers to help me finish

pumping gas. He points
his index finger at the pump
thumb in the air.

No one looks like a shooter.

The Setup

He ate like someone crumpling a piece of paper. I wish
I'd written that line. I closed the book and
tasted that which can't
be recovered from. This quelling took me
to my former office and that of an ex-
boss, the old racist, caught and
sued. His bigotry costs him millions
in sensitivity training for all of us, back in the days
when that was punishment, teaching old
dogs not to get caught.

Finding Work

In the dream, it was almost
too late. I wondered why
I'd never made a career
making crosswords. Not
the kind everyone
knows, but the kind
no one's made
yet. I'm good with grids,
I'm terrible with puns.
I like word acts, speech acts.
I hate impenetrable
puzzles sometimes found
in the *Times*, their smug quips
and privileged clues, caveats
and rare expressions
used in shelved translations
and cryptic best sellers, obscure
ideas meant to make everyone
curious or angry. Both.

Is this how some poetry
works? where
you'll need to know
the first letter of the middle name
of a disgraced prince,
what makes the grass
in the fairy tale glisten?
or the author [trick
question] who drew
that moat, in which part

of the world? What's
another word for tower,
another word for chill,
the complexion of stone
the color of.... No—wait—
these are clues I might need
to secure a job.

Finally—the bolting
and unbolting, where image
meets text, the wall,
of course, navigable
after all. All things are possible
in my puzzles. I was out of work
in the dream, and really did
need to work, so drawing
from life
was essential. In life I deeply
regret time wasted on subjects
I cared little about. The day jobs,
the lost years. Time.
    Eventually—
I found chemistry, work
where the goal
is to make everything
majestic. Every night
I paint squares on a page
before going to sleep,
a letter becomes
a stain. And still
I keep stroking the page,
and still I keep
leaving things out.

To My Day Job

I cheated on you
it's true, day in,
day out, giving you
less than my best
self, making love
to my art, keeping my
heart apart. You had
my body, by day,
every day. I did
what I did
for sanity's sake.
But that's
what they all say
in order to stay.

Brake Lights

When I described
the one thing I adored

about the imported car,
famous

for its hydro-pneumatic
suspension,

the brake light design
—*typical*, my best friend said

to relish the one thing
you'll never see while driving.

Self as Hypotaxis

by which I mean, ego is hierarchical,
X is better than Y. Today
is better than this same day in May

last year. I am happier than I was
when spring equaled death,
so many wakes, so many silences,

equal and un-equal. Spring
sometimes operates
in opposition

to her contract with the earth, and
is not always the birth
of something good. The earth asserts

all seasons be different
but equal. Each a beauty. Maybe
the earth has a preference. Summer,

after all, is generally queen.
I doubt I am alone
in singling out late June

by the sea,
as heaven on earth.
The earth warms,

and not in a threatening way.
The worms brave
the earth's skin's surface

moving through turf
after a rain, free. And even if
it hasn't rained since spring

the flags of my disposition
are happiest in summer, that is to say,
greener, and fresher. And softer longer.

Autobiographia Literaria

after Frank O'Hara

Someday the blank page will rush
under me and with the grace

of a walk in the woods
with you, who have been silent

for years. You will blow sun
in the spring-leafed trees,

and the damp earth
will begin to dry

and crack, and the birds
who no longer migrate

will start to sing, despite
global warming, for they, too

love the author, who stumbles
through time. Still, there's a chance

that history repeating itself
will change course. *You're not*

dead yet, a friend who has
passed liked to say, and

I've been known
to perseverate. And repeat, and repeat,

and will probably do so
from the grave, my stone

etched with the text: Not yet.
Not yet.

The scraps of text on papyrus, dry as dirt, attributed to Sappho, are pinned in place by the tiniest strips of archival tape. I had never seen adhesive so delicate, so *trusted*. The most beautiful thing about trust is what holds it in place.

"non-place" is anthropologist Marc Augé's term for a space of transience, anonymity, that does not hold enough significance to be regarded as a "place"

"he ate like someone crumpling like a piece of paper" is a line from a short story, "Obsession," by Clarice Lispector

"one word bites another," a line from Ray Johnson's notebooks

"like injured fans," from Marianne Moore

"alone and in a circumstance," from Emily Dickinson

ACKNOWLEDGMENTS

I'm grateful to the editors and publishers of the following journals, sites, and anthologies, in which these poems first appeared:

AMP (Hofstra University Press): "Artificial Intelligence," "Next"
Combine Books: "Oh!"
Five Points: "This"
Global City Review: "the most beautiful thing [drive],"
Grayson Books, *Treelines: An Anthology of 21st Century American Poems* (anthology): "Autobiographia Literaria"
Milk & Honey Press, *I Wanna Be Loved By You: Poems on Marilyn Monroe* (anthology): "One Sings, the Other Doesn't"
Cordite Review: "A Thing or Two"
The Night Heron Barks: "Autobiographia Literaria," "One Sings, the Other Doesn't"
Ocean State Review, Tenth Anniversary Issue: "Self-Portrait as Hypotaxis"
On the Seawall (ronslate.com): "How to Draw a Heart," "Fuel," "Inventory," "Now," "Caper," "The Motorist," "Finding Work," "The Setup"
Plume: "Copper Beech," "A Singleton," "Self-Portrait: Between the Car and the Sea"
Rattle: "Anthem"
Sheep Meadow Press: "Drive" (excerpted from) Prospect/Refuge
Upstreet: "Driving," "Landscape with Power Lines," "Sky Burial," "Sew"
What Rough Beast? Poets Respond to the Election, 2016: "On Rothko's 'Dark Palette'"

My thanks to Rebecca Allan, Joan Cappello, Ruth Danon, Patrick Donnelly, Billy Hands, Jessica Greenbaum, David Groff, Luke Johnson, Laura Kaminsky, John Kramer, Kaye McDonough, Teddy Laurel, Amy Lemmon, Daniel McCusker, Roger Mitchell, Frances Richey, Heather Sellers, Ron Slate, Jennifer Stewart Miller, Jeet Thayil, Lynne Thompson, and Michelle Valladares. I'm grateful to my colleagues and staff at the Sarah Lawrence Writing Institute, the writers of 2 Horatio, the Urban Rangers, and for the time and space afforded me to work on this book at the home of Emmanuelle Huisman-Perrin and Bruno Perrin (Paris), and residencies at the Siena Art Institute and time at Arts Workshop International (Assisi). And a special thanks to Elizabeth Murphy, the extraordinary editor of this book. And to Katherine Bradford, whose artwork makes a poem of the cover of this book.

DEDICATIONS

"Caper" is for Ron Slate

"Copper Beech" is for Nora Conant

"How to Draw a Heart" is for Ken Mills

"Listening to Cement Dry" is for Bonnie Jill Emmanuel

"Old. Rome." is for Kaye McDonough

"One Sings, the Other Doesn't" is for Teddy Laurel

"sin·gle·ton" is for John Kramer

"Sky Burial" is for Cynthia Van Hazinga

"This" is for Heather Sellers

ELAINE SEXTON is the author of three previous collections of poetry including *Sleuth*, *Causeway*, and *Prospect/Refuge*. She currently teaches at the Sarah Lawrence Writing Institute and lives in New York City and the North Fork of Long Island.